safe

strong

important

I am
Brave

loved

free

Yvonne Martinez

I am Brave

ISBN-13: 978-1505544275

Printed in the United States of America

Recommended Brave Workbook Supply List

Each girl should receive their Brave workbook inside a nice color gift bag with the following supplies for the lessons.

- **8 1/2 x 11 White or pastel gift bag containing:**
  - **I am Brave workbook**
- **8 ½ x 11 Large plan white envelopes for Treasure Envelope**
  - **Pen**
- **10 sheets of 8 ½ x 11 Multi-colored construction paper cut in 1/4ths to use as cards throughout the lessons.**
- **Tongue depresser or large craft stick for face mask handle**
  - **Glue stick**
  - **1 set Crayons or colored pencils**
  - **Sharpener**
  - **Scissors**
- **3 x 4 Small zip lock filled with 30-40 multi-size gem stones and**
  - **3-4 different colors of 1' length cuts of narrow ribbon**

In addition, group leader should have:

- **A bag of multi-colored pompoms or cotton balls**
  - **Hole punch**

Have fun!

About the Author

Yvonne Martinez

Yvonne is Director of Transformation Center, Bethel Church, Redding, CA, where she helps to oversee 30 counselors and Transformation Center's program development. She is the founder/director of CARE-EDU (Center for Advanced Recovery Education), an Internationally Certified Alcohol and Drug Counselor, and author of 14 books including:

- *Dancing on the Graves of Your Past book, workbook, advanced, and group leader's guide*
- *I am a Woman-Healing the Feminine Spirit book and workbook*
- *Prayers of Prophetic Declarations*
- *Prayers of Prophetic Declarations for Teens*
- *Prophetic Gates*
- *Addictive Personality*
- *Healing the Self-Harm Associated with Trauma*
- *I am Brave, a Workbook for Girls*

(See back of workbook for contact information)

I am Brave

Your experience isn't your identity.

Your history isn't your destiny.

I am Brave

I am Strong

I am Safe

I am Loved

I am Important

I am Powerful

I am Free

I am Me!

Hello from Yvonne!

My name is Yvonne and I am writing this workbook for you. This workbook is for those who are beginning their journey to restore their dignity, identity, and destiny. Included are principles I have used for years with others I've helped find healing from painful experiences.

The chapters in this workbook may seem simple at first, but they will bring you deep healing because they connect you with Jesus, who is the healer. When Jesus healed my broken heart, he told me that I would be used to help others. It was true!

You might be wondering about what happened to me growing up, and I don't mind sharing my story. My parents were alcoholics. I was hurt by them and by other people, too. I experienced emotional, physical and sexual violation. I didn't have a voice or any choices as to what I wanted or needed. I carried shame and rejection because of what happened to me, and I even hurt myself because I didn't feel important or loved.

That all changed when Jesus restored my dignity, identity, and destiny. Today, my life is completely different. My broken heart and pain are gone and I am no longer ashamed of my past. I am free!

I have counseled and prayed for thousands of women and written several books and workbooks. My life has been dedicated to helping women, and I believe, with all my heart, it is not by chance that you are reading this letter.

Jesus wants you to know something very important!

Your experience isn't your identity.

Your history isn't your destiny.

You are Brave

You are Strong

You are Safe

You are Loved

You are Important

You are Powerful

You can be Free to be YOU!

John 3:16

For God so loved the world, that He gave His only Son, Jesus, that whoever believes in Him should not perish but have eternal life.

About I am Brave Workbooks

I am Brave workbooks are interactive, so you will be coloring, drawing, writing and using scissors. You will also be taking out of the workbook all the good things you will want to keep as a reminder of how much you received through I am Brave lessons.

- ♥ The workbook is experiential.
- ♥ There is no right or wrong answer to the questions.
- ♥ There is no pressure to participate.
- ♥ Have fun!

Important!

❖ Decorate your Treasure Envelope.

When you see this mark, it is your clue to follow the instructions!

➢ Leader's instructions

When you see this mark, it is instruction for your leader.

➢ **Let's get started!**

♥ You have a large white envelope.

♥ This is your personal **Treasure Envelope**.

♥ Your Treasure Envelope is a special place to keep all the good and positive things you will receive during the lessons.

❖**Decorate your Treasure Envelope!**

I am Brave

1 Corinthians 16:13

Watch, stand fast in the faith, be brave; be strong.

Beauty-Bear

This is my own beautiful bear. I have had her for a very long time.

My bear was designed and sewn together by a friend as a gift for me. I call her my Beauty-Bear! She is actually made from old clothes that belonged to family members. The outside fabrics are pieces from my grandmother's apron, my sister's dress, my brother's shirt, my mom's blouse, etc. The design is called "patchwork" because it represents pieces (or patches) of different fabrics that are sewn together.

Our lives are like patchwork designs, too. We are made of bits and pieces of our dad, mom, grandparents, and ancestry that represent a mixture of experiences, family, culture, and beliefs.

Like the patchwork "skin" of Beauty-Bear, our family, culture, beliefs, and experiences shape who we are. But, on the inside, we are made special, specific, original, unique, individual, and we all have different gifts, talents, strengths, creativity, and dreams.

❖ You have a Beauty-Bear, too!

❖ On the next page draw and decorate your Beauty-Bear.

❖ **Decorate your Beauty-Bear here.**

❖ **Decorate inside the lines.**

What is Bravery?

Bravery is the ability to do something that you know is right or good, and also to face something that is very difficult, painful, or dangerous.

Being brave doesn't mean that we are not confused, worried, or afraid, but bravery can help overcome our fear when we are willing to protect something or stand up for something in which we believe.

Bravery is what compels a fireman to run into a burning building. While he knows the danger is real, it is his duty to face that danger.

When soldiers go to war, they fight because they love what they are defending.

Around the world, brave men and women are honored in acts of service and recognized for their contribution.

Recognized Badges of Bravery

United States Medal of Honor - Awarded for acts of heroism in extremely dangerous situations at risk of life above and beyond the call of duty while engaging an enemy.

Purple Heart - Awarded for wounds suffered in combat, often while saving others.

<u>Bronze Star Medal</u> - Awarded for heroism or meritorious service in the midst of active combat.

<u>The Victoria Cross</u> - The highest military award that may be received by members of the armed forces in the British Army for extraordinary courage "in the face of the enemy."

The <u>Param Vir Chakra</u> - The highest military award in India given to those who show the highest degree of valor or self-sacrifice in the presence of the enemy.

<u>The Profile in Courage Award</u> - A private award that is given to recognize displays of courage. It is given to individuals (often elected officials) who, by acting in accord with their conscience, risked their careers or lives by pursuing a larger vision of the national, state or local interest in opposition to popular opinion or pressure from others or other local interests.

People who are Famous for Grand Acts of Bravery

- <u>Harriet Tubman</u> leading slaves to freedom on thr Underground Railroad.
- <u>The Pilgrims</u> coming to the United States without any idea of what they were about to face.
- <u>Anne Frank</u> and her family living in secret and quiet to hide from the Nazis.

- The policemen, firefighters, and citizens who rushed into buildings to save lives when the Twin Towers were attacked in New York on September 11, 2001 .

- Charles Lindbergh making the first nonstop flight in a blimp across the Atlantic ocean from New York to Paris.

- Mother Teresa living amongst the poorest of the poor and helping them to learn and grow.

- Sir Edmund Hillary climbing up Mount Everest.

- People working for safety and peace with worldwide movements such as the Red Cross, and the Peace Corps.

- Women and men who put their lives at risk to change laws and fight for rights for women and those who work to end human trafficking and slavery.

All of these people put themselves at risk in order to do what they thought or felt was right.

Jesus Christ is the bravest person ever. He showed extreme bravery to follow His faith, beliefs, and mission despite being accused, rejected, brutally beaten, nailed to a cross and left to die. Jesus' acts of bravery were because He loved His Father, God, and the people in the world. He was brave and did this for you and me so we could be free. Jesus gave His life because of love.

Bravery allows people to do what is required when doing good or battling evil.

Bravery is not the absence of fear. Bravery is the resistance, suppression, or detachment from fear to push forward and get the job done.

In most cases, people who are honored with a Badge of Bravery suffered great distress in completing their task or assignment. The Badge of Bravery acknowledges the person's heart, mind, or body may have been wounded in the effort of being brave.

Firefighters who race into a burning building to save lives are certainly brave, but sometimes the biggest act of bravery is a small one. Brave people do acts of bravery every day, even if their acts of bravery aren't noticed by others.

People who endure hardship, loss, or a traumatic experience are examples of some of the bravest people on the planet. They don't usually think of themselves as brave, but they are. You are brave right now!

When soldiers return home, however, they have a difficult time lowering the bravery they used to perform their duty. When they return from war, the defenses they created to protect themselves are the same defenses they must lower to return to a life of freedom.

Even when soldiers have the confidence to know they can stand and fight, they still may worry that without their bravery they may be unsafe or afraid. The longer they fight in battle, the longer they wear their bravery and repress the fear.

To the brave, taking their armor off may feel like the act of a coward, when it is really a true act of courage. But many soldiers returning from war keep the bravery on. This may trap and hold in their emotions and delay their destiny, which can lead to isolation, depression, anger, addiction, or self-harm.

But it is not just soldiers, fire fighters, and policemen, for example, who become trapped by bravery -- it can be anyone who is required to be brave and repress their fears to "get through it" or "get the job done."

When you learn that bravery protects you, it is hard to risk putting bravery down. We keep our bravery on because we are defending what is in the inside of us, too. It can keep us protected from feelings or emotions but can also keep us away from our creativity, dreams, and destiny.

Courage helps brave individuals release the feelings and emotions they keep bottled up. Courage is the ability and willingness to confront fear, pain, danger, uncertainty, or intimidation.

It takes courage to do what is right when facing fear, shame, gossip opposition, or discouragement.

Acts of courage happen every day. Because we live in a world where people experience difficulties, you'll probably recognize some of the following acts of courage.

Everyday acts of courage:

- Trying a food that you've never tried before
- Being open to change
- Engaging in a new experience
- Asking someone to be a friend
- Confronting a bully
- Allowing yourself to feel what you're feeling
- Doing something that might be a little risky such as riding a bike for the first time
- Standing up for a person who is being picked on
- Trying a new task or job
- Walking down a dark road at night
- Looking in the mirror with kindness
- Helping out a person or animal in need, even if it might put you in a little bit of danger
- Standing up for yourself
- Writing your own story
- Leaving an abusive relationship
- Trusting someone
- Sharing your opinion
- Singing a song
- Doing something by yourself for the first time

- Signing up for a new program or class
- Making a public presentation about something you believe in
- Saying kind things about your self
- Standing up against injustice
- Running from danger
- Following your heart
- Setting boundaries
- Letting go of people who let you down
- Risking loving someone
- Letting someone love you
- Dancing
- Trusting your creativity and dreams
- Asking for help

❖ Circle the statements that reflect your courage.
❖ Can you think of others, too?
❖ Write them here.

braver

is about the courage it takes to live your life well.

It's not about skydiving or bungee jumping.
It's about taking a leap—or even a tiny little step—
toward the person you most want to be.

❖ **Who is the bravest person you know?**

❖ **What did they do to show bravery?**

❖ **Ask Jesus if you ever needed to be brave.**

❖ **What did he show you?**

❖ **Write on a card about your bravery.**

❖ **Place finished cards inside your Treasure Envelope.**

❖ **Ask Jesus what He thinks about your bravery.**

❖ **What did He show you?**

❖ **Write it on a card and then place the card inside your Treasure Envelope.**

➤ **Leader, explain about badges of bravery a different way if your group's culture doesn't understand or doesn't recognize badges of bravery and/or if the police and public officials were not safe people in their community.**

❖ **What would your personal badge of bravery look like?**

❖**Draw and decorate
your personal badge of bravery here.**

❖**Cut it out and put in your
Treasure Envelope.**

My Heart

You notice my Beauty-Bear has a heart, just like you and me. Experiences can change the way we feel about ourselves and others. Experiences can hurt our heart, our mind, and our body. We might feel afraid, alone, and unprotected.

Someone hurt me. It felt like an arrow pierced my heart, and I was worried, anxious, afraid, ashamed, alone, unsafe, and unprotected.

This was my heart before Jesus healed me. This is what trauma felt like to me.

❖ If your heart hurts,

draw a picture of how it looks or feels.

❖ **Ask Jesus how He feels about your heart.**

❖ **Write what He shows you on a card.**

❖ **Place finished cards inside your Treasure Envelope.**

❖ **Ask Jesus what He wants to do to help your heart. Write on a card what He shows you.**

❖ **Place finished cards inside your Treasure Envelope.**

❖ **Cut out the drawing of your badge**

❖ **Cut out the drawing of your heart**

❖ **Save these in your Treasure Envelope.**

I am Strong

Philippians 4:13

I can do all things through Him who strengthens me.

Strong-Bear

There are different ways we can be strong. Bravery helps to be strong toward things outside, and courage helps us be strong on the inside.

♥ It takes bravery to be certain and strength to have doubts.

♥ It takes bravery to fit in and strength to stand out.

♥ It takes bravery to hear a friend's pain and strength to feel our own.

♥ It takes bravery to guard and strength to let down our walls.

♥ It takes bravery to conquer and strength to surrender.

♥ It takes bravery to stop abuse and strength to endure.

♥ It takes bravery to stand alone and strength to lean on a friend.

♥ It takes bravery to love and strength to be loved.

♥ It takes bravery to survive and strength to live.

We are born with personal strengths that demonstrate our unique design. These are strengths of character that a person owns, celebrates, and frequently exercises. Our personal strengths are always with us but sometimes we don't recognize that we have them.

Everyone is special and expresses their strengths according to their unique personality. Next are examples of personal strengths.

❖ Notice how you feel when you read each description and circle the ones that feel like "YOU".

Personal Strengths

♥ **Curiosity/Interest in the World:**

You are curious about everything. You are always asking questions, and you find all subjects and topics interesting. You like exploration and discovery.

♥ **Love of Learning:**

You love learning new things, whether in a class or on your own. You have always loved school, reading, and museums-anywhere and everywhere there is an opportunity to learn.

♥ **Critical Thinking/Open-Mindedness:**

Thinking things through and examining them from all sides is an important part of who you are. You are not quick to form opinions, and you rely only on trustworthy evidence to make your decisions. You are able to change your mind.

♥ **Creativity/Practical Intelligence:**

Thinking of new ways to do things is a very important part of who you are. You are never content with doing something the traditional way if a better way is possible.

♥ **Emotional Intelligence:**

You are aware of the motives and feelings of other people. You know what to do to belong in different social situations and you know what to do help others feel comfortable.

♥ **Wisdom:**

You may not think of yourself as wise, but your friends would say that you are. They value the way you see things and ask you for advice. You have a way of looking at the world that makes sense to others and to yourself.

♥ Valor and Bravery:

You are a courageous person who does not turn away from threat, challenge, difficulty, or pain. You speak up for what is right even if someone disagrees. You do what you believe is right.

♥ Endurance:

You work hard to finish what you start. No matter the job, you finish it on time. You do not get distracted when you work, and you take satisfaction in completing tasks.

♥ Honesty:

You are an honest person, not only by speaking the truth but by living your life in a genuine and authentic way. You are a real person who is not afraid to be yourself.

♥ Kindness and Generosity:

You are kind and generous to others, and you are never too busy to do something for someone. You enjoy doing good things for others, even if you do not know them well.

♥ Loving and Allowing Oneself to be Loved:

You value being close with others, especially those in which sharing and caring are given as well as received. The people to whom you feel most close are the same people who feel most close to you.

♥ Loyalty:

You are an excellent member of a group. You are a loyal and dedicated teammate, you always do your share, and you work hard for the success of your group.

♥ Fairness and Equity:

Treating all people fairly is very important to you, and you try to do so all of the time. You do not let your personal feelings affect your decisions about other people. You give everyone an opportunity.

♥ Leadership:

You excel at what is needed for leadership: encouraging a group to get things done and keeping harmony within the group by making everyone feel included. You do a good job organizing activities and seeing that they happen.

♥ Self-Control:

You purposefully control what you feel and what you do. You are a disciplined person. You are in control of your appetites and your emotions; they do not control you.

♥ Discretion:

You are a careful person, and your choices are consistently wise ones. You do not say or do things that you might later regret.

♥ Humility and Modesty:

You do not ask to be noticed, preferring to let your actions show for themselves. You do not think of yourself as better than anyone else, and others recognize and value your modesty.

♥ Appreciation of Beauty and Excellence:

You notice and appreciate beauty, excellence, and/or skilled performance in all areas of life, from nature to art to mathematics to science to everyday experience.

♥ **Gratitude:**

You are aware of the good things that happen to you, and you are always thankful for them. Your friends and family members know that you are a grateful person because you always take the time to express your thanks.

♥ **Hope:**

You expect the best in the future, and you work to achieve it. You believe that the future is something to look forward to with enthusiasm and goals.

♥ **Spirituality/Sense of Purpose:**

You have strong and reasoned beliefs about the higher purpose and meaning of the universe. You know where you fit in the larger picture. Your beliefs shape your actions and are a source of comfort to you.

♥ **Forgiveness and Mercy:**

You forgive those who have wronged you. You always give people a second chance. You operate out of mercy and not revenge.

♥ **Playfulness and Humor:**

You like to laugh and tease. Bringing smiles to other people is important to you. You try to see the humor in all situations.

♥ **Enthusiasm:**

No matter what you do, you approach it with excitement and energy. You never do anything halfway or halfheartedly. For you, life is an adventure.

How do we know when a particular strength is ours?

- **a sense of ownership ("this is the real me")**
- **a feeling of excitement while displaying the strength**
- **looking for opportunities to use the strength**
- **wanting projects that give opportunity to use the strength**
- **pursuit of activities that revolve around the strength**

❖ **What strengths do others see in you?**

❖ **If you are not sure, ask a friend or your group to tell you what they see about you.**

❖ **When you hear what they say, does it feel true to you?**

> Surround yourself with the dreamers and the doers, the believers and thinkers, but most of all, surround yourself with those who see greatness within you, even when you don't see it yourself.

❖ **After reading the list and asking someone who knows you, close your eyes and ask Jesus to show you what strengths He most loves about you.**

❖ **Mark the strengths that He shows you.**

❖ **Do you feel these are true about you?**

❖ **Which one do you like the most about you?**

❖ **Write them on one of your cards.**
❖ **Place finished cards inside your Treasure Envelope.**

When we have to be brave to protect ourselves or someone else, we may hide our strengths. Sometimes our true strength hides until it is safe to be seen.

❖ **Do you have strengths that you feel were hidden?**
❖ **Write them here.**

Living in our strengths is an example of being "real" and shows others who we are.

❖ What strengths are safe to been seen by others?
❖ Write them here.

You might realize by now that bravery is something we "do" and strength is something we "are."

When we can let down our bravery, our strengths help us to connect with our heart, with others, and with Jesus. Our strengths help us to be "real" without pretending, performing, or protecting.

It seems easy to just stop pretending, performing, or protecting and just be "real," but often it isn't easy or simple to do.

For example, warriors taken captive by an opposing side may be forced to obey their captors. They might submit to the captors' demands on the outside by showing bravery, but on the inside they are really very kind and caring, wise or creative. Sometimes the fear or worry over what's happening forces us to restrain and hold back our true strengths and we have to behave in ways that isn't the real "us."

This doesn't just happen in war. It can happen with people we know and with strangers. Sometimes we may do things that are against our beliefs or morals because it is necessary to stay safe. Sometimes we might be told a lie or tricked.

It doesn't mean that you wanted or liked what happened. It means that someone's will for you was stronger and more forceful than you or your needs.

When warriors or firemen are brave, they get to wear protective armor to help them be safe.

Armor-Bear

When you were afraid or in danger, you may not have had a tough outside armor like Armor-Bear to keep you safe. When you were brave, you may have had to wear a different kind of armor. Your armor may have been the face you showed on the outside, the way you talked, the way you behaved, or what clothing you wore. It is a way we pretend to be different than we really are so we can be safe.

Here are a few examples of how I wore a type of armor when I was in danger.

- I was quiet. Quietness made me feel it would help me not to draw attention to myself.

- I agreed with what someone wanted. Agreement made me believe it would keep me safe from someone's anger.

- I had to be still. Stillness made me feel safer because it might stop me from getting hurt.

- I didn't care. Not caring helped me to disconnect from pain that was in my heart.

Wearing this kind of armor made me appear different on the outside than how I really felt on the inside.

Like the armor I wore, armor can be something as simple as a face expression that conveys a message to others. I was like Pretend-Bear, wearing a mask, so no one could see inside me.

We pretend to be someone different on the outside than we are on the inside. We feel safe as long as we believe others can't see what's on the inside of us. It is like wearing a mask.

Pretend-Bear

On the next page are some examples of masks that you might wear.

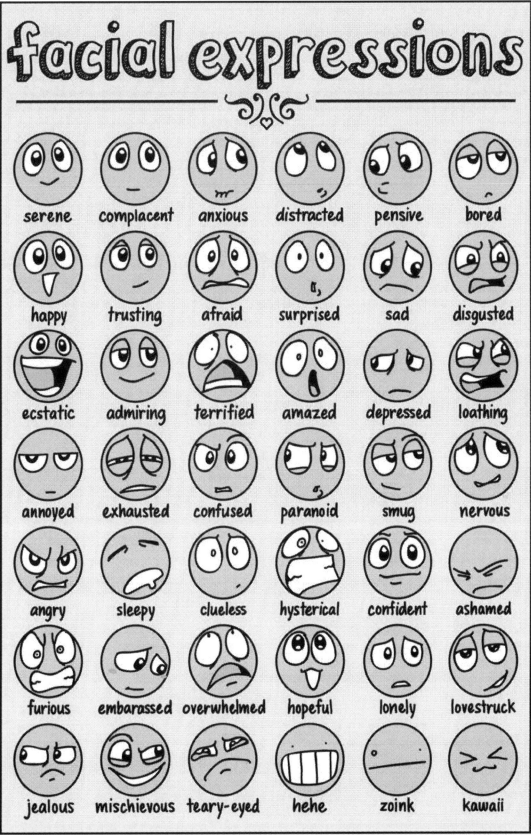

❖ **Did you ever wear a pretend face (mask) that helped you hide what was inside?**

❖ **Draw what your pretend face (mask) looked like.**

❖ Cut out the mask and glue to stick.

Glue the stick high enough onto the back of the mask to hold the paper firm after it is cut out.

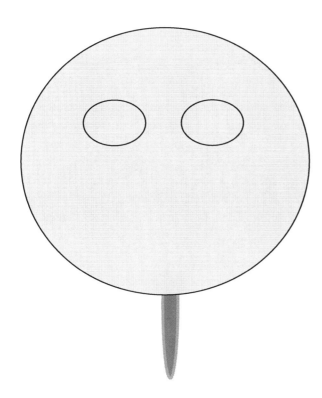

❖ What is your mask's name?

❖ Do you have more than one?

❖ **When do you need to put in on?**

❖ **How do you feel when it is on?**

❖ **How does it help you?**

❖ **How does it hurt you?**

❖ **When your mask is protecting you, where does your heart go?**

➢ **Leader, Father God always gives us a way of escape and sometimes our brave armor and masks are gifts from God to help us survive difficult situations.**

PRAY and thank God for allowing brave armor and brave faces that helped protect us when we needed them.

I am Safe

Psalm 138:7

Though I walk in the midst of trouble, you preserve my life. You stretch out your hand against the anger of my foes; with your right hand you save me.

Safe-Bear

The person in protective armor perceives themselves as now being safe. But the armor is just a disguise, a mask that gives the illusion of safety. At best, it is a false security and something we can control.

A pretend face might actually work to push people away, to hide sad feelings or protect your heart, but it also holds out joy, peace and emotional freedom, dreams, and a new fun experience.

No one can decide for you when it is safe to take off put the mask, to put it away, to visit your heart or express what is inside of you, or when to access your real strength, creativity, and dreams.

There are three ways you might know if you are safe without keeping the mask.

1. When you feel it no longer protects you.

2. When you don't need or want it any longer.

3. When something else will keep you safe.

When you are ready to put bravery aside, lay down your armor, and look under the mask, it will require courage, but you won't have to do it alone.

While most people just want to forget what happened and move on, they can't stop the memories and experiences from popping up. This is what PTSD does. Sometimes the memories are loud and penetrating, and other times can be quieted or ignored.

Feelings of rejection, betrayal, hatred, anger, and unforgiveness are natural feelings from being hurt. But when we hide our heart, the feelings and our behavior can hurt us or someone else. Internal conflicts might feel worse when we detach from our feelings.

We needed a brave armor of self-protection to survive neglect or violence. But later in life, those behaviors can become the walls that close us in and keep everyone else out. Our armor of self-protection becomes the wall that blocks intimate relationships.

Like the soldiers returning from the war who need to lower their brave armor, we will need to lower our armor to experience real freedom to be who we are created to be.

Taking our armor off can expose the pain underneath. That is why courage is needed. But it is the only way you will know who you really are.

Keeping the memories alive helps people who are hurting to prove the validity of what happened. You may be the only witness to the trauma or who can testify to the trauma's reality.

Why do the actions from those who hurt you hold so much power over us and have the ability to make us feel guilt or shame for what someone else did to us? Shame leaves you hopeless because there is nothing you can do about believing the misconception of "I am a mistake." Some of us are clothed in shame, a deep feeling of uncleanness, and this can lead to self-hatred. Shame is rooted in the fear of abandonment and rejection.

It sounds silly to think that someone hurts you and you feel it is your fault. But it is possible to assume responsibility for others by agreeing with statements like, "It must have been my fault." Believing it was your fault is a type of false power—that you had the power to make someone behave a certain way.

You may be holding yourself responsible for the actions of others. Assuming responsibility for others is "false guilt." No matter how hard you try, you cannot get rid of the guilt and shame that belongs to someone else --- because it was never yours to begin with!

Shame and fear are both forms of control, focusing on something other than authentic feelings.

❖ You can separate true responsibility from false responsibility.

Finish with your own list.

TRUE I AM responsible for:	FALSE I AM NOT responsible for:
I left my purse at the store.	Someone stole my money.
I talked to a stranger.	The stranger hurt me.
I went to work.	They didn't let me go home.
I drank a glass of water.	Someone put drugs in my water.
I made a wrong decision.	Someone forced me to have sex.

Keeping a secret is very powerful.   As long as the secret stays hidden, you feel in control.

The secrets and things you have done can be surrendered to Jesus, and He forgives all our sins when we ask.   But maybe the biggest barrier is you forgiving yourself.   Holding on to the pain of our mistakes prevents us from our dreams and destiny because we get stuck in our pain and shame.

What can you give to Jesus?
- ♥ **You can give Him mistakes.**
- ♥ **You can give Him bad choices.**
- ♥ **You can give Him things that hurt someone.**
- ♥ **You can give Him responsibility for other people.**
- ♥ **You can give Him pain.**
- ♥ **You can give Him fear.**
- ♥ **You can give Him shame.**
- ♥ **You can give Him doubt.**
- ♥ **You can give Him secrets.**
- ♥ **You can give Him worries.**
- ♥ **You can give Him sadness.**
- ♥ **You can give Him suffering.**
- ♥ **You can give Him your armor.**
- ♥ **You can give Him your mask.**
- ♥ **You can give Him whatever you don't want any more.**

When we surrender to Jesus, he always gives us something better in exchange. He always trades up! Isaiah 61:3 gives us an example of His exchange system. When we give Him the things that we don't need or want, He gives us better things.

- ♥ **We give Him ashes, He gives us a crown of beauty.**
- ♥ **We give Him mourning, He gives us the oil of joy.**
- ♥ **We give Him despair, He gives us a garment of praise.**

❖ **Ask Jesus what is safe to give to Him right now.**

❖ **Would you like to give this to Jesus now?**

❖ **If you give these things to Jesus, ask Him what is He going to give you in exchange?**

❖ **Write what you want to give to Jesus around the edges of page 15, beside (not on) your Beauty-Bear.**

❖ **Go ahead and begin cutting out your Beauty-Bear as you give these things to Jesus. You are cutting off and giving to Jesus all the things you don't want.**

➢ **Leader, pray out loud, calling out things which could be given to Him.**

❖ **Ask Jesus what He wants to give you in exchange.**

❖ **What did He give you? Write it on a card.**
❖ **Place finished cards inside your Treasure Envelope.**

❖ **Receive the exchange He gives you.**

❖ **How do you feel with all these things gone?**

❖ **Write on a card the good feelings. Be sure to put all your cards in your Treasure Envelope.**

❖ **Add new Beauty-Bear to your Treasure Envelope.**

If you would like to, you can ask Jesus to let you use some of His strength. This is also how you can reduce anxiety and fear and help you be more confident to look inside your heart and to use your real strengths every day.

Would you like to access Jesus' strength to help you?

1. Receive Jesus and His strength

Jesus comforted His people while he was on earth, but when he died and went to Heaven, he sent another comforter called the Holy Spirit. This word "comforter" means to run toward us, to run by our side and pick us up.

The Bible tells us that the Holy Spirit will be with us forever, to comfort us, teach us and help us to know the truth.

John 14:15-17…And I will ask the Father, and he will give you another advocate (comforter) to help you and be with you forever— the Spirit of truth. The world cannot accept Him, because it doesn't see Him or know Him. But you know Him, for he lives with you and will be in you.

2. Receive the Holy Spirit

3. Walk through finding Jesus' Kingdom of God inside you by using Psalm 16:1.

Psalm 16:1 "Keep me safe, O God, for in you I take refuge...."

4. Close your eyes and look inside you to find the Holy Spirit.

❖ **The Holy Spirit feels warm and fuzzy, soft, quiet, playful, real and fun, just like colorful pompoms or cotton balls.**

➢ **Leader, do pompom toss**

I am Loved

Romans 8:38, 39

For I am convinced that neither death nor life, neither angels nor demons, neither the present nor the future, or any powers, neither height nor depth, nor anything else in all creation, will be able to separate us from the love of God that is in Christ Jesus our Lord.

Loved-Bear

L is patient.
is kind.
does not envy.
does not boast.
is not proud.
is not rude.
is not selfish.
is not easily angered.
keeps no record of wrongs.
does not delight in evil.
rejoices in truth.
always protects.
always trusts.
always hopes.
always perseveres.
never fails.

{1 Corinthians 13:4-8}

This is real love. God describes love in great detail in the Bible in the verses from 1 Corinthians 13:4-8.

Let's take God's love and apply it to a human relationship.

What if a person who loved you...

- ❖ Responds with patience, kindness, and is not envious of you?

- ❖ Is not boastful or prideful?

- ❖ Is not rude toward you or self-seeking or easily angered?

- ❖ Does not keep any record of your wrongs?

- ❖ Refuses to be deceitful and is always truthful with you?

- ❖ Protects you, trusts you, always hopes for your good, and perseveres through conflicts with you?

- ❖ Does not want you for sex and treasures every moment you spent with them?

- ❖ Makes plans with you for your future and desires you to prosper in all you do?

- ❖ Provides unlimited creativity and wisdom?

- ❖ Can understand and know what you need, answering and responding before you can ask?

- ❖ Gives you a full partnership, power and authority to rule in the kingdom they own?

This is how God defines His love and the intimate connection He wants us to experience. He describes love that is giving, rather than self-seeking. And there's the problem: What human can live up to this?

Most women have never felt pursued, loved, or adored for who they are. They never felt acknowledged or where they belong. They have never felt they are worthy of someone sacrificing their life so they could live free.

Sometimes we feel unworthy, ashamed, fearful, or even angry. Sometimes we feel we can't trust others and can't trust ourselves.

This is why God's love is so powerful, NOTHING can separate us from God's love. That is because God's love is IN us. We are made in God's image and God is love (1 John 4:8).

You are created in the Image of Love. No one EVER can change the truth. You ARE loved and love is in YOU!

Love is active. Freedom requires you to embrace love, activate it, and then to give it away.

Real love actually brings justice and protection.

BEING DEEPLY
LOVED
BY SOMEONE GIVES
YOU STRENGTH
WHILE LOVING
SOMEONE
DEEPLY GIVES
YOU COURAGE.

❖ **When our heart is hurt, it doesn't feel loved.**

The open place in the picture is where something or someone invaded into your safe place of protection. When this happens, we don't feel loved. We might not know where or how to find love again. Fear is the enemy of love.

If we can't find love, it can feel very unsafe. Jesus said that when we feel unprotected or unsafe it feels like our heart is an orphan, just left alone and abandoned without any help. When our heart feels orphaned, it feels like it can't find love. Our heart can feel like it is in a prison.

❖ **Would you like to receive God's love?**

❖ **Ask for the Spirit of Adoption**

➢ **Leader, you can pray to release Spirit of Adoption.**

❖ **Place your hand on your heart and receive....**

❖ **Decorate your Certificate of Adoption.**

❖ **Add your name and todays date.**

❖ **Cut out and put in your Treasure Envelope.**

Kingdom of God

Certificate of Adoption

Date: _____

This certificate is awarded to
(Your name here)

_____

I am Brave

I AM
THE DAUGHTER OF A KING WHO IS NOT MOVED BY THE WORLD FOR MY GOD IS WITH ME & GOES BEFORE ME I DO NOT FEAR BECAUSE I AM
HIS

This is Papa-Bear. You look just like Him!

You look just like the one who created you! You are created in the image of a good God who loves you. He gave you a place in His heart.

❖ **Put your hand on your heart and ask Papa God if you are safe right now.**

❖ **If the answer is YES, ask Papa God if it is okay to look in your heart to discover your real strengths, dreams and destiny?**

❖ **If YES... Cut out Papa Bear and tie your Beauty-Bear close to Papa Bear.**

❖ **Put in your Treasure Envelope.**

Papa-Bear and YOU!

❖ **How do you feel being close to Papa Bear?**

Notice that Papa God accepts you even if you are sad, or have armor, or masks. He accepts you. But He knows, if you will let Him protect you, you may be happier and free without them. He is giving you an to let Him protect you instead.

❖ **Put your hand on your heart and ask Papa God if it is safe now to look under the mask and inside your heart.**

You can't change what someone said or did to you, but you can give the leftovers to Jesus and you can let go.

Forgiveness

God provided forgiveness for people who were destined to fail but who chose to return to God. God sent His son Jesus who for all time *is* the sacrifice for our sins. It is through Jesus we have forgiveness, and because we have been forgiven we can forgive others.

Unforgiveness keeps the door open to the pain of trauma. It also leaves the door open to anger, hatred, bitterness, and self-harm. Holding onto unforgiveness can cause us to feel in control.

Strings of unforgiveness keep us connected to painful experiences, bad feelings, and harmful people.

The person or situation that hurt you has moved on, and we are left feeling stuck with what they did to us. Our feelings of bitterness, revenge, hatred, anger, or self-harm actually hurts us inside.

Bitterness

Revenge

Hatred

Anger

Self-Harm

The only way to get unstuck and unhooked from someone who hurt you is to forgive them and then you can get your heart healed.

Forgiveness is a fruit of surrender. Those who surrender their lives to God choose to forgive, not because they should, but because they want to. Forgiveness is the courage to let mercy triumph over judgment (James 2:13).

Giving forgiveness to those who hurt us

When we experience the grace of God's forgiveness we can forgive others more easily. We choose to release from our judgment those who have hurt us, and we choose to show mercy toward them. Releasing others from our prideful judgment releases us from the pain and emotional torture unforgiveness produces. When we forgive, God releases us, and we release ourselves.

Think of a fish caught on a hook. As the fish struggles and struggles, the hook penetrates deeper into the fish. As long as the fish focuses on the fisherman and the struggle, the hook twists and turns in its flesh. The struggle causes more pain for the fish than for the fisherman. When the fish forgives, it cuts the line and stops the struggle with the fisherman. Forgiveness sets the fish free. Afterward, the fish can get the hook out, allowing the wound to heal.

Giving forgiveness to those who are not sorry

Often we want to set up conditions or see remorse on someone's part before we will forgive them. Sometimes we want them to "suffer the consequences" of their behavior, so we withhold forgiveness. This really means our forgiveness is conditioned upon the guilty party's repentance. We say, "*If you're sorry, I'll forgive you.*" Jesus says, "*I forgive you,*" which causes us to feel sorry. Jesus' forgiveness and mercy invites our repentance. When we forgive, we let go of our connection to their behavior. This actually allows the other person freedom to wrestle with their own broken heart.

Giving forgiveness when you don't feel like it

When hurt hasn't been addressed, forgiveness will seem detached from feelings.

It is like looking into a closet that has been cluttered for a long time. Every time you open the closet door you see the mess and feel bad. You will never enjoy the good feelings that come from having a clean closet while you are still looking at the mess. Just as soon as you begin working on the mess and the closet is finally clean, the good feelings of relief and release come naturally.

When you obey God and clean out the clutter of unforgiveness, you are drawn closer into the next dance —the Dance of the Overcomer.

Giving forgiveness to those who persist in abusing you

Whoever hurts you or abuses you, a Christian, is guilty of sin against God's temple (1 Cor. 3:16; 6:19). Allowing them to continue hurting you is not good for them and, of course, is not good for you. In every case that Jesus endured or submitted to persecution, it was to bring glory to His Father. Likewise, our submission should bring glory to God or cause others to be drawn to Christ.

When David was persecuted and pursued by Saul (1 Samuel), he removed himself from the violence. On two occasions, David spared Saul's life when he could have killed him in defense. If David had retaliated, he would have been no better than Saul. David was able to leave Saul in God's hands, and God honored David.

Relationships that continue to damage you emotionally or physically need to be handled with the same maturity. You can remove yourself from the abuse and the abuser. Forgiveness doesn't mean you can or should continue in relationship with people who aren't safe or aren't trustworthy.

Giving forgiveness when you are angry

Being angry is not a sin, but extended hostility, insult, or injury is. Anger has active expressions like yelling, throwing things, or hitting people. It also has passive expressions like forgetfulness, procrastination, or apathy. You know anger is a sin when you see its negative responses and reflection in the faces of others we have hurt.

Asking forgiveness for our offenses

When we confess our sins (and unforgiveness is a sin), God will forgive us. This forgiveness is guaranteed through Jesus. When possible, we also need to ask for forgiveness from those we have directly or indirectly hurt.

What Forgiveness Isn't

Forgiveness isn't denying the pain

Sally was taken into the woods and tortured by a boyfriend. Sally managed to get to the road and was rescued by a driver. Forgiveness doesn't erase Sally's need for medical attention. The brutal physical wounds from Sally's attack aren't healed when she forgives her attacker. There remains the process of learning how to live her life in the aftermath of this tragedy. Forgiveness is essential, but we may be faced with physical and emotional pain that needs further healing to put lives back on track.

In the fishing story, after the line was cut, the hook in the fish still needed to be removed so the wound could heal.

Forgiveness isn't excusing what they did

My husband, Tony, led a prison ministry. Every service he ministered to men who were forgiven by Christ, yet who were still serving their sentences. Forgiveness repairs the spiritual judgment, but it doesn't necessarily absolve from the restitution required according to our moral, judicial, or governmental laws.

Forgiveness isn't reconciliation

Forgiving doesn't mean you will, or can, have relationship with the ones you forgive.

My father died before I became a Christian. Forgiveness couldn't reconcile our relationship, but I have the peace of knowing I let go of my hurt and anger. Through Christ, I was able to forgive him for his rejection and abandonment.

Forgiveness isn't reconciliation, but it's a beginning

Returning to the fishing story, we need to cut the line, remove the hook, and get help for our wounds. During this process we learn valuable lessons about where the fisher fishes and what bait he uses. Learning healthy boundaries helps to ensure we activate the tools needed for building safe relationships.

Relationship with the fisherman may not be possible or safe, but we will swim along happier because forgiveness will help us.

❖ **Can you forgive the people who hurt you?**

❖ **Who are they?**

❖ **Can you give to Jesus what happened to you or to someone you loved?**

❖ **What do you need to give to Jesus?**

❖ **If Yes...pray through forgiveness**

❖ **Ask Papa God if he will protect you if you cut the string and release the people who hurt you.**

❖ **When you are ready, cut the string and let them go.**

➢ **Leader, help pray.**

❖ **How do you feel now?**

❖ **Ask Papa God what He wants to give you in exchange. Write it on a card and put it in your Treasure Envelope.**

Jesus died so our sins, mistakes, and shame would no longer be connected to us (2 Cor. 5:21). His Cross is where that happened. Our sins, our mistakes, our shame, and our bad choices are all erased at the Cross. Romans 6—the death of Christ wipes out, cancels, and erases the record of our old nature.

❖ **Papa God is with you.**

❖ **Can you forgive yourself?**

❖ **If yes, take your Beauty-Bear from your Treasure Envelope.**

❖ **Look at your Beauty-bear and forgive yourself.**

➢ **Leader, help pray.**

❖ **How do you feel now?**

❖ **Write it on a card and put don't forget to put it in your Treasure Envelope.**

❖ **Ask Papa God what He wants to give you in exchange and write it on a card.**

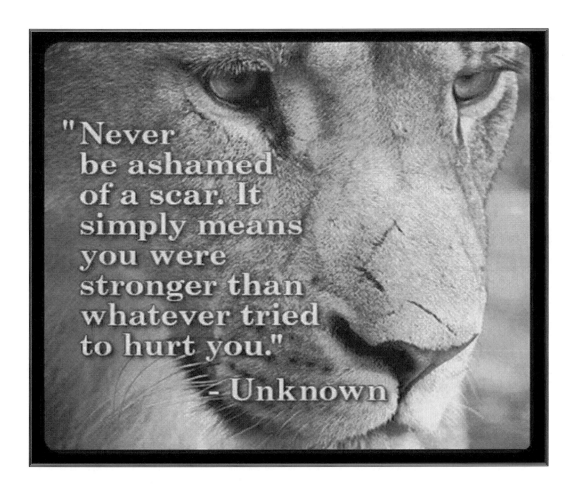

"Never be ashamed of a scar. It simply means you were stronger than whatever tried to hurt you."
— Unknown

Jesus wants to give you a new heart.

❖ **Would you like a new heart?**

❖ **What would it feel like?**

❖ **What would it look like?**

❖Decorate your new heart.

❖Cut your new heart out of the workbook.

❖ **Would you like to exchange your new heart for your old, hurting heart?**

❖ **If Yes, take the old hurting heart out of your Treasure Envelope.**

➢ **Leader, pray out loud and thank Jesus that He gives us a new heart!**

❖ **Put your new one in your Treasure Envelope**

❖ **Tear up the old one!**

IT DOESN'T REALLY MATTER WHO I USED TO BE. ALL THAT MATTERS IS WHO I HAVE BECOME.

❖ **Communion = Co-union is becoming more aware of being ONE with Jesus.**

➢ **Leader, you can offer communion with emblems and scriptural significance.**

❖ **Is there anything you want to tell Jesus?**

❖ **Is there anything He wants to tell you? Write it on a card and put the card in your Treasure Envelope.**

I am Important

Ephesians 1:18

I pray that the eyes of your heart may be enlightened in order that you may know the hope to which He has called you...

"Promise me you'll always remember that you are braver than you believe and stronger than you seem and smarter than you think!"

Focusing on our strengths and our passions helps us to find our purpose in life and live out our destiny.

❖ **What do you love to do? These would be the things you are passionate about.**

❖ **Write 5 things you are passionate about.**

1.

2.

3.

4.

5.

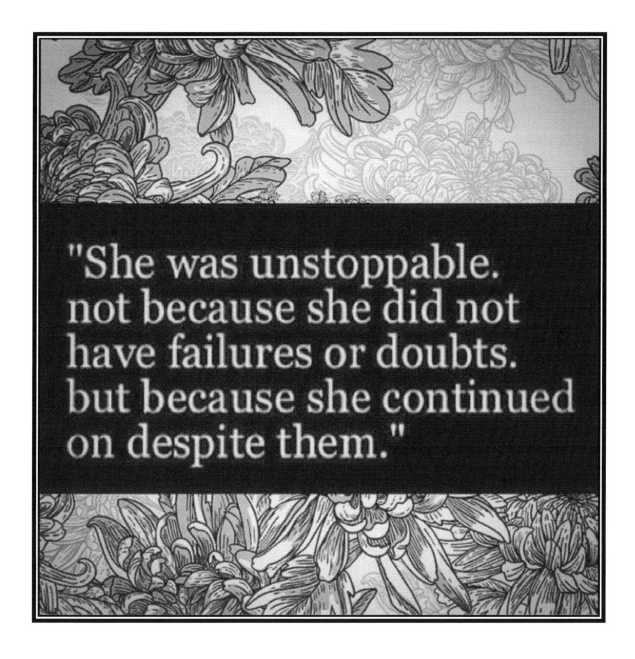

"She was unstoppable. not because she did not have failures or doubts. but because she continued on despite them."

Finding your Purpose

Step 1—Look at the list of your strengths. On the next page list the strengths that describe you. You can list all of them that apply to your own life.

Step 2--List your passions. List your specific passions. Passions are the things that you love to do in your life, even if you actually have done them yet or not. Passions can also be the dreams and destiny that you envision for yourself later in life.

Strengths + Passions = Purpose

Try it ...

Example:

My strength is Wisdom	Expressed through my love (passion) of
♥ Others value the way you see things and ask you for advice. You have a way of looking at the world that makes sense to others and to yourself.	Teaching children in school.

Strength

Passion

My Strength is	Expressed through my love (passion) of

Step 3 --Design your purpose statements. Take your strengths and associated passions and place them into a sentence that describes a path toward your destiny.

❖ *My desire and purpose in life is to express*

[Strengths]

_____

through my love of

[Passions]

_____.

❖ **My desire and purpose in life is to express**

[Strengths]

_____

through my love of

[Passions]

_____.

❖ *My desire and purpose in life is to express*

[Strengths]

_____

through my love of

[Passions]

_____.

❖ **My desire and purpose in life is to express**

[Strengths]

_____

through my love of

[Passions]

_____.

❖ *My desire and purpose in life is to express*

[Strengths]

_____

through my love of

[Passions]

_____.

❖ **Cut your destiny statements out of the workbook and put them in your Treasure Envelope.**

I am Powerful

Ephesians 2:6

And God raised us up with Christ and seated us with Him in the heavenly realms in Christ Jesus...

Powerful-Bear

God's love is always **powerful** and willing to make us a better person. I am a powerful person when I can love God, others, and myself.

Papa God thinks we are awesome! He lends us His strength and power so we can be successful in life.

We can learn to manage ourselves so others don't need to control us.

Boundaries

Boundaries establish limits. Good boundaries help keep us safe and help us to pursue our strength and passions.

Not setting boundaries is a lack of self-protection usually based on fear. Unhealthy boundaries are the result of poor self-esteem. The first step in establishing healthy boundaries is to believe you are worth protecting and have the right to be safe.

Weak Boundaries

If you have weak boundaries, you will often do anything for other people as you may be fearful or feel guilty to say "no." You lack a definite line of where your personal responsibility ends and other people's responsibility begins. You could often be seen as 'a follower.' If you have weak boundaries you may also blame others for your misfortunes and you may feel others are responsible for maintaining your emotions and behaviors. Also, you may not respect the boundaries of others.

Signs of weak boundaries

* Accepting responsibility for other peoples actions and responses

* Focusing on other people

* Being too responsible or irresponsible

* Giving away your power or taking too much power

* Having no sense of privacy in a relationship

* Invading others' rights sexually

* Emotionally dependent

* People-pleasing

* Feeling confused

Healthy Boundaries

If you have healthy boundaries, you can regulate your own reality. This means that you can choose what you want in your life and also what is not acceptable. In addition, you are able to communicate these needs to those around you. You will also take responsibility for your own behaviors and not take on other people's problems.

It's also about you knowing what you want from others, what you will or will not accept from others, and understanding how you want to be treated. However, the most important part of learning to implement healthy boundaries is to first believe that you deserve to be treated well and to activate a new set of beliefs about what you believe are your rights as a child of the King. This protects your authentic identity.

In essence you need to believe and know your Kingdom identity. Once you have this priority in place, healthy boundaries will feel natural.

External Boundaries

Interpersonal boundaries are about what you will accept from others. They are the limits we set with those around us based on certain people, times, and places. They are about what behaviors we will accept from other people and those that we will not accept.

Internal Boundaries

Internal boundaries are about what you will accept for yourself. Internal boundaries include knowing your own beliefs, values, thoughts, feelings, and attitudes. They are about the decisions and choices you make for yourself and the experiences you participate in.

Boundary Gates

Boundary gates are opened two ways.

- **They open from the outside in.**
- **They open from the inside out.**

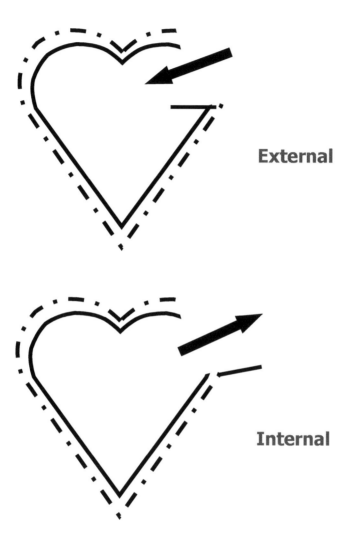

External

Internal

Often adults who were hurt as children lack the ability to set appropriate boundaries.

A person hurt as a child may have learned early on that setting boundaries conveyed resistance or refusal to submit, which only enraged the abuser and caused more rejection or abuse. In these situations, not having boundaries, limits, or protective resistance may appease the abuser, stall the violence, or deflect the abuser's anger, diminish the abuse, or even seem to initiate peace.

Shame is intensified when I feel...

- I should have or could have prevented the abuse/trauma
- I am at fault

❖ **Have you carried responsibility for what someone else did, such as the words they spoke, their actions, or their behavior?**
❖ **If YES, then ask Jesus if it is time to let the responsibility go.**

➢ **Leader, pray to release responsibility and belief they have the power to make a person speak or behave a certain way.**

A Princess in God's Kingdom!

We are His chosen, His friend, the object of His affection and attention. This is not only freedom from your past but freedom to engage your destiny.

In Song of Songs 2:9,10 the "lover" comes to the "beautiful one" to arouse her from a place of comfort. The lover invites the beautiful one out from behind her wall to join Him as he, like a gazelle, bounds from mountain top to mountain top. We join Him as a partner with our hand in His hand and close by His side.

Accepting the invitation means she must come out from behind her wall.

"But we all, with unveiled face, beholding as in a mirror the glory of the Lord, are being transformed into the same image from glory to glory, just as by the Spirit of the Lord." (2 Cor. 3:19)

The veil (any protective covering) needs to be removed so we can go from "glory to glory."

He doesn't break down the wall or rip off the veil. He doesn't kidnap her against her will. Rather, it is a partnership whereby she willingly joins Him. Accepting the invitation, He begins to teach her about conquering and overcoming, dominion, and authority.

❖ **Are you ready to receive your Princess crown of royalty?**

❖ **If yes, are you ready to let go of any armor, mask, or wall that would block you from your destiny?**

❖ **If you are ready, you can give Jesus your mask.**

❖ **If you know there is more than one pretend face, then add the names to the mask.**

➢ **Leader, help pray.**

❖ **You can tear it up the mask and exchange it for a Princess crown of royalty!**

❖ Cut out and decorate your Princess crown.
❖ You can wear your Princess crown!

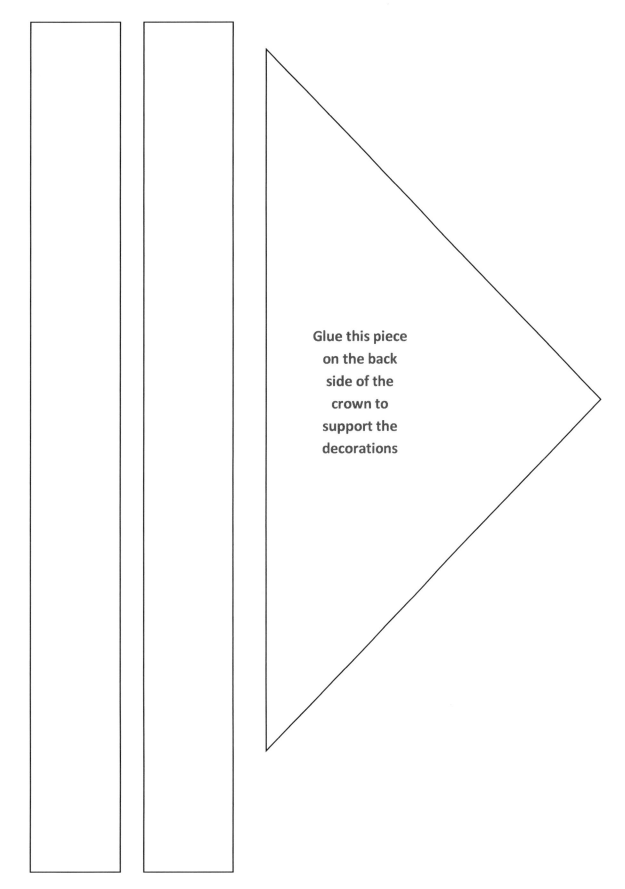

Glue this piece
on the back
side of the
crown to
support the
decorations

I am Free

Galatians 5:1

It is for freedom that Christ has set us free. Stand firm, then, and do not let yourselves be burdened again by a yoke of slavery.

Free-Bear

Jesus believes in us. He wants us to be free to express our unique strengths and style.

❖ What does freedom mean to you?

❖ In what ways would you like to express your freedom?

❖ Write or draw your "expression of freedom" on a card and put in your Treasure Envelope.

what if
I fall?

oh, my
darling,
what if
you fly?

I love the story of Jairus' daughter in the Gospel of Luke 8:41-54. Jairus requested Jesus come and heal His daughter who was ill. By the time Jesus arrived at Jairus' home, everyone was crying because, from all outward appearances, the daughter had died.

Jesus led the faithful past the faithless and went into the room where the daughter lay. He made a declaration..."*she is not dead, but asleep*!" Jesus followed up the declaration with a prophetic act, grasping her hand and telling her to get up!

God pushes past the unbelievers, those who hurt us and those who gave up on us. He pushes beyond our past and pain, and, as His daughters, declares we are not dead, just asleep.

❖ **Is there a part of you that needs to be awakened to life?**

➢ **Leader, pray through the following:**

o **break soul ties**

o **break off trauma**

o **body ownership exercise**

o **restoration of innocence**

o **bless spirit and give mother's blessing**

I am Me!

Colossians 2:9-10

...you are complete in Him, who is the head

of all principality and power.

Me!

Proverbs 31:25

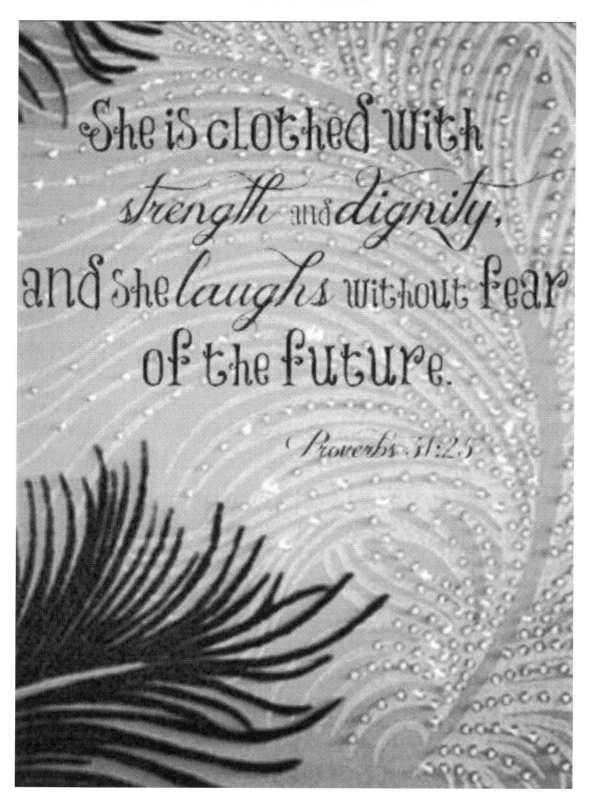

I am Brave!

❖ **Celebrate by decorating how you are clothed in strength and dignity, without fear of the future.**

❖ **Cut out and put in your Treasure Envelope.**

❖ Let's read out loud together!
You can cut out the poem and put in your Treasure Envelope.

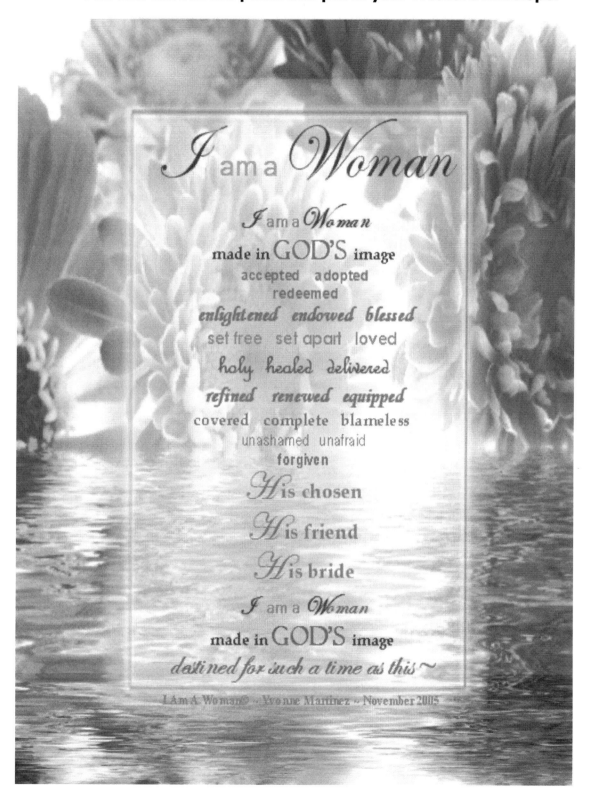

I am a Woman

I am a Woman
made in GOD'S image
accepted adopted
redeemed
enlightened endowed blessed
set free set apart loved
holy healed delivered
refined renewed equipped
covered complete blameless
unashamed unafraid
forgiven
His chosen
His friend
His bride
I am a Woman
made in GOD'S image
destined for such a time as this ~

I Am A Woman © ~ Yvonne Martinez ~ November 2005

❖ **Now it is time to open your Treasure Envelope and see all the beauty, creativity, strength, love, hope, passion, and dreams that are uniquely YOU!**

Everyone reflects a facet of God.

Acknowledge each other's uniqueness, too.

❖ **Ask the Holy Spirit for encouraging words for someone.**

❖ **Write what He gives you on a card and give the card to that person.**

➢ **Leader to officiate adoption ceremony.**
❖ **Adoption Ceremony**

❖ **Write your dreams on a card.**

❖ **Write your destiny, calling, what you love to do, and what makes you come alive!**

❖ **Write on a card the testimony of what Jesus has done for you. Put it in your Treasure Envelope.**

❖ **Create a new song!**

❖ **Ask the Holy Spirit for words to a new song in your heart. Write them on a card for your envelope... AND write the words inside this music box, too!**

❖ **Cut out the words from your new song and set aside for the final activity.**

❖ **Say out loud together...**

My experience isn't my identity.

My history isn't my destiny.

I am Brave

I am Strong

I am Safe

I am Loved

I am Important

I am Powerful

I am Free

I am Me!

❖ **Cut this declaration out of your workbook and put inside your Treasure Envelope.**

> ➢ **Leader, what is left in the workbook is an old identity. It is now time to make the greatest exchange of all.**
> ➢ **During the "Arise" ceremony, each person will come forward and leave their old identity at the cross and return to call the next girl to arise, by helping her up.**
> ➢ **Leader, pray for each girl as they do this.**

> ➢ **Leader starts ceremony to arise.**

> ❖ **Ceremony to Arise**

Arise!

Believe in Jesus

Believe in yourself.

> ➢ **Leader, while everyone is standing...**

> ❖ **Get in a circle.**
> ❖ **One at a time, each person sing out their words.**
> ❖ **When finished, all together you have written (and sang!) a new song from the Lord!**

For more information

I am Brave workbooks and training

Visit the website

www.iambrave.info

Yvonne's online store
shop.yvonnem.org

Yvonne Martinez CADCII, ICADC

CARE-EDU
1095 Hilltop Dr., #243
Redding, CA 96003

Transformation Center, Bethel Church
20 Lake Blvd Redding, CA 96003

yvonnem@ibethel.org

yvonne@care-edu.com

www.iambrave.info

yvonnem.org

Made in the USA
Middletown, DE
28 February 2023

25774834R00086